This Ladybird book
belongs to

....

For Brenda. You have welcomed so many children
into your home with love and understanding, irrespective
of their background. Your kindness and heartfelt
approach will never be forgotten.
L. H. A. MBE

To Tarsila, my Dublin older sister, who welcomed
and guided me during my first years so far from home,
whose love I am so grateful to have in my life.
G. M.

LADYBIRD BOOKS

UK | USA | Canada | Ireland | Australia
India | New Zealand | South Africa

Ladybird Books is part of the Penguin Random House group of companies
whose addresses can be found at global.penguinrandomhouse.com.
www.penguin.co.uk www.puffin.co.uk www.ladybird.co.uk

Penguin
Random House
UK

First published 2023
001
Written by Laura Henry-Allain MBE
Illustrated by Giovana Mederios
Copyright © Ladybird Books Ltd, 2023
Printed in China

The authorized representative in the EEA is Penguin Random House Ireland,
Morrison Chambers, 32 Nassau Street, Dublin D02 YH68

A CIP catalogue record for this book is available from the British Library
ISBN: 978–0–241–61048–0

All correspondence to:
Ladybird Books, Penguin Random House Children's
One Embassy Gardens, 8 Viaduct Gardens
London SW11 7BW

MIX
Paper from
responsible sources
FSC
www.fsc.org   FSC® C018179

MY FAMILY
YOUR FAMILY

Written by
LAURA HENRY-ALLAIN MBE

Illustrated by GIOVANA MEDERIOS

We all have a family.

But what *is* a family? The word **family** means a group of people who are connected.

Every family is **unique**.

Sometimes, this means grown-ups who have a child or children.

It could mean people who share the same surname . . .

or people who live together in the same home.

Your family can live with you or near you, in the same country or in a different country.

Family members can feel like friends, and they can make us happy, sad or angry.

Our families can even include our pets.

What does "family" mean to you?

How many people live with you?

Is it noisy or quiet where you live?

Do all your family members live with you?

Some people think a family is a mum, a dad and two children, but, when we think about our own families and look at our friends' families, we can see that . . .

EVERY family is different!

People in your family are called your **relatives**. They may be related to you by blood, marriage, court orders or adoption. Relatives who are part of your closest family could be your . . .

mum

dad

stepdad

half-sister

half-brother

stepsister

Families can come together and grow together in different ways. Some people might think only a mum and dad can have a child, but this is not the case. There are lots of ways grown-ups might have a baby!

One way is a process called "surrogacy". This is when a grown-up, known as a "surrogate", grows a baby in a "mummy tummy" for another grown-up or a family. The surrogate becomes pregnant and has a baby for the new parent or parents.

Another way is a process called "donorship". This is when a grown-up gifts, or donates, sperm or an egg (natural parts that make a baby) to another grown-up or family so that they can have a baby.

If a donor makes more than one donation to the same family, the children are related and might be known as **diblings**.

Your family might be bigger than just you, your siblings and your parents. You might have relatives who are part of your wider, or extended, family. The names for these relatives can be:

uncle

adoptive family

cousin

aunt

nephew or niece

childminder

foster family

grandmother, grandfather, great-grandmother or great-grandfather

You may have a special name for one or more of your relatives. For example, in Saint Lucia a godmother is called a "nennen".

godmother or godfather

Sometimes, a community can also feel like family. Some people consider their friends or neighbours to be their family. Community groups can be . . .

sports teams

religious or faith groups

nurseries or schools

dance groups

When we talk about family, we might draw, write or make special marks to show who is in our family and how we are all connected. This is called a family tree.

grandad   grandma   grandpa   nana

mum   dad   aunt   uncle   uncle

sister   brother   baby   cousin

My mum's brother is my uncle.

My mum's gran is my great-grandmother.

My dad's new husband is my stepdad.

My sister and I love to read books together.

My dad had a car accident and uses a wheelchair. Sometimes, my siblings and I support and take care of him.

My uncle's daughter is my cousin.

My foster mum is called Fatima.

Over the years, families can change for many reasons.

A new baby or child might come into the family.

A family member might die.

A parent might meet a new partner or partners.

Parents might separate and no longer live together. If they are married or have a civil partnership, they might get a divorce or a dissolution.

Two or more families might come together to create a blended family.

A child might be adopted by a grown-up or a couple, or be adopted into a different family.

A grown-up or a family might decide to foster a child or foster more children.

A grandparent, older sibling, friend, aunt or uncle might create a kinship family with a child. This is when a relative looks after a child in place of a parent. They might live in the relative's home or the child's home.

Some children can become carers for their parents or siblings. This may happen if someone in a family becomes ill, or if a parent is unable to properly care for themselves and is therefore unable to care for their children.

Change can make us feel happy, sad, upset or excited.

It is important to talk about how you feel with a grown-up you trust.

Some children live in a blended family.

Sometimes, a couple who are married and have children might not get on any more. They could separate, decide not to see each other or get a divorce.

I live with my dad from Monday to Friday. Then I live with my mum from Friday to Monday.

One of them may choose to remarry or live with another grown-up. The new grown-up becomes a step-parent to the children.

I didn't want my own children, but now I have a bonus son!

If a step-parent already has children, a big blended family is created, and the children become stepsiblings.

In my family, I don't call him my stepbrother. I call him my brother!

If the parents of a blended family decide to have a child, then that baby will be a half-sibling to all the children, because half-brothers and half-sisters share a parent.

Me, too. I call my half-sister my sister!

Some children live in adoptive and foster families.

When a child is unable to live with their birth family, social workers will step in. They will take the child to a safe place where grown-ups look after children, such as a children's home, the home of another member of the child's family or into care with foster carers. The child will be looked after for a few weeks, months or years, or until the child becomes a grown-up.

There are many reasons that children are taken into care. A child's parents might die, or their parents and extended family might not be able to look after them.

Children in care are sometimes fostered. This means that they live with local-authority-approved grown-ups in the grown-ups' home, and they can stay there for a short or long time. Foster children are legally looked after by the local authority until they are adults.

Some children are adopted. This happens when someone who is not a birth parent legally becomes a child's parent.

Some children are adopted at birth, some are adopted by a parent's new partner, and sometimes children are adopted from care, either by their foster family or different grown-ups. Children who are adopted live with the grown-ups who adopted them as their child.

Children who are fostered or adopted have birth parents and birth families. They might know who they are, or they might not.

It's important to remember that they are still part of a family.

The place a family lives is called a home. Homes come in all different shapes and sizes. They can be found in lots of different places, such as busy cities, quiet towns, canals or the middle of the countryside.

Where do you live?

Do you live in a city, a town or the countryside?

What does your community look like?

What things do you do in your home?

What is your home like?

Some families spend a lot of time together, and others can't or don't spend any time together at all. Family time can be fun, stressful, difficult or relaxed. Families might . . .

play games

eat

laugh

visit new places

have fun

share their feelings

dance

sing

go for a walk or a run

Do you spend time with your family?

What things do you do with your family?

What is your favourite thing to do with your family?

Are there any things you would like to do with your family?

What languages do you speak with your family?

Some families only come together at special times called **celebrations**. They might support and celebrate each other, and they may do this . . .

on a birthday.

as part of a religious or non-religious festival or celebration, such as Baisakhi, Hanukkah, Diwali, Christmas, Eid al-Fitr, Pride, Lunar New Year or Emperor Selassie's birthday.

to celebrate special events like adoption anniversaries or naming days.

to remember a family member who has died.

at a special community event, such as a carnival, horse fair, street party or barbecue.

to support a family member who is doing something special, like singing in a choir, playing in a cricket match or performing in a school play.

Do you celebrate with your family?

Do your celebrations include any special music, food, clothing or decorations?

Are there any traditions that you and your family do together?

Do you have a favourite holiday or celebration?

What did you last celebrate with your family?

Every family is different.

No two are the same.

Families come in different sizes – some are small, and some are big with lots of relatives.

No matter what a family looks like,
it's the love within it that counts.

Glossary

adoption: the legal process that a grown-up or couple uses to become the legal parent(s) of a child

birth parents: a child's biological parents

blended family: a family with a number of parents, which may include half-siblings and stepsiblings

carer: a grown-up or child who cares for another grown-up or child

children's home: a local-authority- or privately-owned house, where children of different families live together and are looked after by grown-ups

co-parenting: when parents both care for a child following a separation. The child lives between the different homes of their parents.

diblings: children who have the same donor parent and live in the same family

divorce: when two grown-ups who were married go through a legal separation and are no longer together

extended family: another name for a wider family unit, including relatives such as grandparents, uncles, aunts and cousins

foster parent: a government-approved grown-up who looks after a child for a short or long period of time

half-sibling: someone who shares one parent with you

heritage: part of a person's culture, for example, the language, tradition and knowledge that is passed on

kinship family: a child who is cared for by a grandparent, an adult sibling or another relative, such as an aunt or uncle, is part of a kinship family

local authority: a group responsible for providing services and making decisions about what is to happen within a particular area of the country

orphan: a child whose parents have died

partner: a name for a grown-up in a relationship with another grown-up. They are each other's partners.

relative: someone in your family who is connected to you, usually by marriage or blood. They may or may not be a traditional family member.

sibling: someone who shares two parents with you

social worker: a professional person who helps lots of different people with their problems. They might help children, the elderly and disabled people. This type of help is referred to as social services.

stepsibling: someone who becomes your sibling when one of your parents and one of their parents become partners or marry

surrogacy: the process of having a baby for another person, couple or family

tummy mummy/parent: another name for a surrogate who gets pregnant for another person, couple or family

Questions

Who do you have in your family?

Can you think of some words to describe your family?

Who is the oldest and who is the youngest in your family?

What is the best thing about being in your family?

A note for adults reading this book

Use this book to enhance the conversations you have with your children about their own family and other families.

Here are some things you may use alongside this book.

- Use photographs to aid memories when talking about family members. For example: "This is your stepmum." or "This is your great-grandmother." Support your child to share their understanding by talking, drawing, using special marks or writing about their family.

- Use memories to recall family events. "I remember when my mum married my stepmum." "Do you remember the party we had to celebrate moving into our new home?"

- When talking about family heritage and where each parent and/ or extended family may have come from, support your child's understanding of geography by using maps and atlases.

- You know your child best, and you will know when you need to have sensitive conversations with them to explain their family and origins. It is important to use the correct terms with children.

- Share a range of books and play materials celebrating different families, and use these as a discussion point. Libraries and toy libraries can be especially useful resources.

- When sharing information about your child with others, you may wish to use a child-centred approach and include the following information: things that are important to your child, key family members, special names you may use for family members, and how the person can support your child.

My family is special to ME!

Laura Henry-Allain MBE is a producer, storyteller, educationalist and consultant. She is the creator of the *JoJo & Gran Gran* characters and is the author of *My Skin, Your Skin*.

Giovana Medeiros is a freelance illustrator from Brazil, now based in Lisbon. She studied Fashion Design, but later pursued her illustration studies at BCFE in Dublin, and has been working as a freelancer ever since. She is very passionate about drawing people and fantastic scenes, and she has worked on children's books from publishers around the world.

The author would like to thank Ann Marie Christian, a safeguarding and child-protection expert with Child 1st Consultancy Ltd, and Lisa Smith, member of the Advisory Council for the Education of Romany and Other Travellers, for their insight and advice on this book.

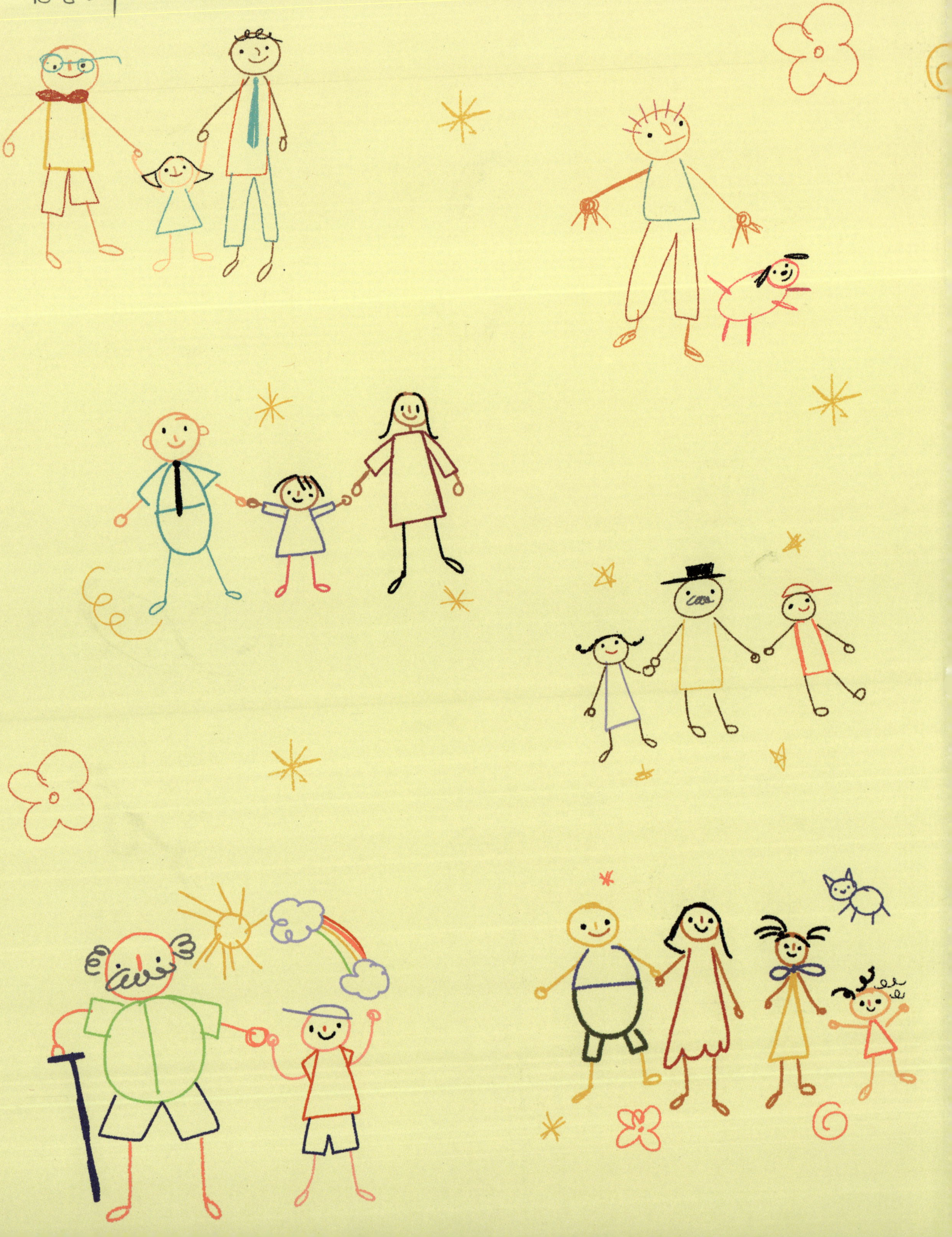